The BASEBALL Alphabet Book

by Stephanie S. Ellis

Dedicated to my brother-in-law Andy Krivonak who spent his life coaching boys and girls to love baseball as much as he did.

To my son, Michael Vienne whose expertise in sports helped me pull it all together, to Loraine Ellis Vienne who is my true inspiration and

TO ALL YOUNGSTERS WHO PLAY BASEBALL
AND TO THE PARENTS AND COACHES WHO
ENCOURAGE THEM IN THEIR SPORT.

All rights reserved. This book, or parts thereof, may not be reproduced in any form without permission in writing from the publisher.

Copyright, 2015 by Stephanie S. Ellis and Mackenzie Woods Publishing

Library of Congress Cataloging-in-Publication Data
Ellis, Stephanie Shriber,
The BASEBALL Alphabet Book / Stephanie Shriber Ellis p 47
An overview of alphabetical terms and pictures pertaining to baseball ...
Paperback   ISBN 97809898118 4 2
1. BASEBALL ---Educational, Juvenile literature , picture book
[1. Baseball] 1. Title

Published in the United States by Mackenzie Woods Publishers
Printed in USA
First Edition 1

Mackenzie Woods Publishing
www.soccerpals.com

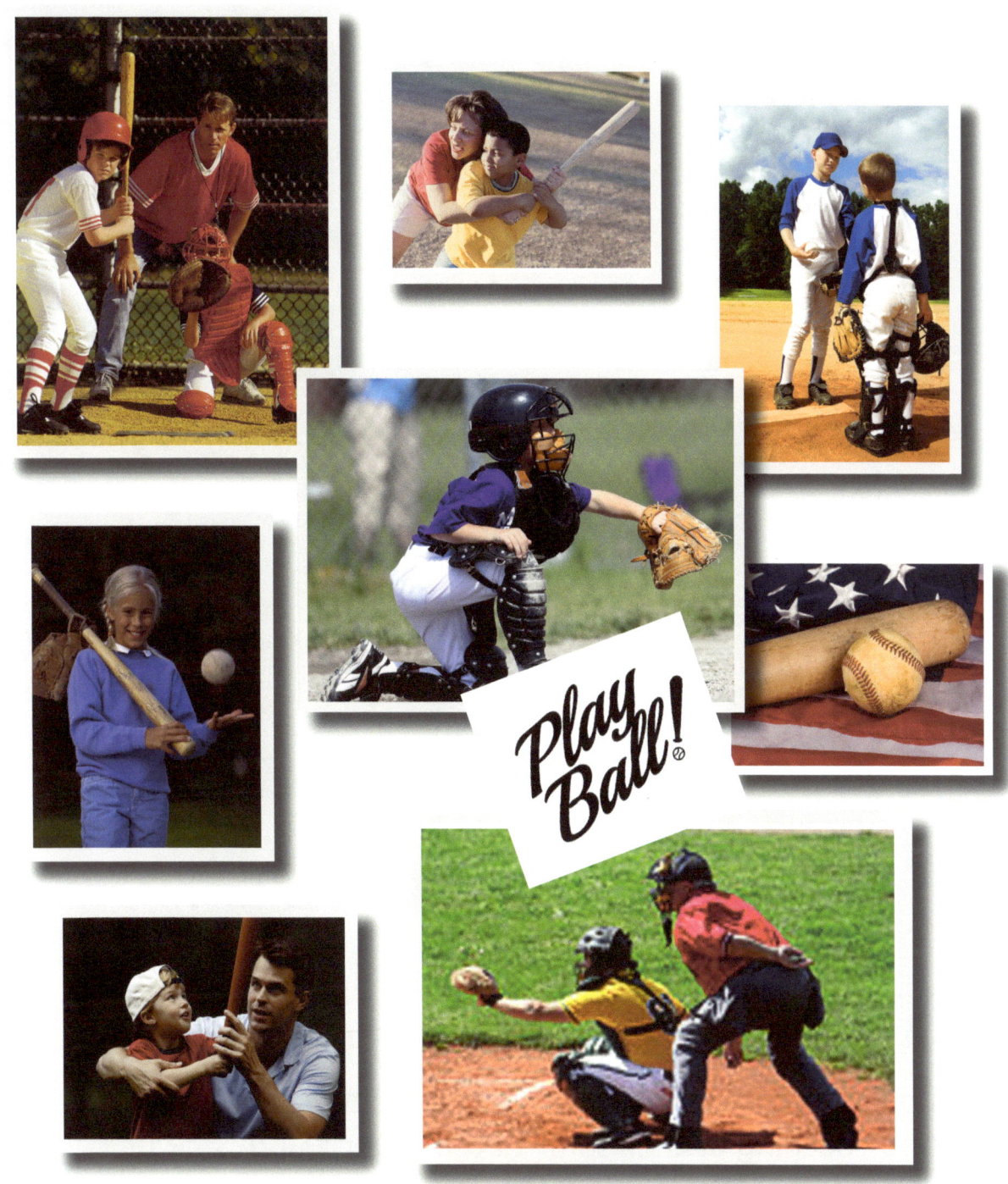

A

ASSISTANT COACH

An assistant coach helps with the team management and coaching of the team. In the lower leagues he or she is very often a volunteer parent.

ACE
The top pitcher on the team is called an ACE.

AWARDS

ADVANCE
When a hitter moves a runner at least one base or when a runner moves along the base lines this is considered advancing.

B

BALL PARK

All ball parks are different but the one thing that they have in common is that they are laid out so a line from home plate runs straight through the pitchers mound and on to second base, east-northeast so that the batters do not have the afternoon sun in their eyes.

BAT

A bat is a tool or stick made of aluminum or wood used to hit the ball.

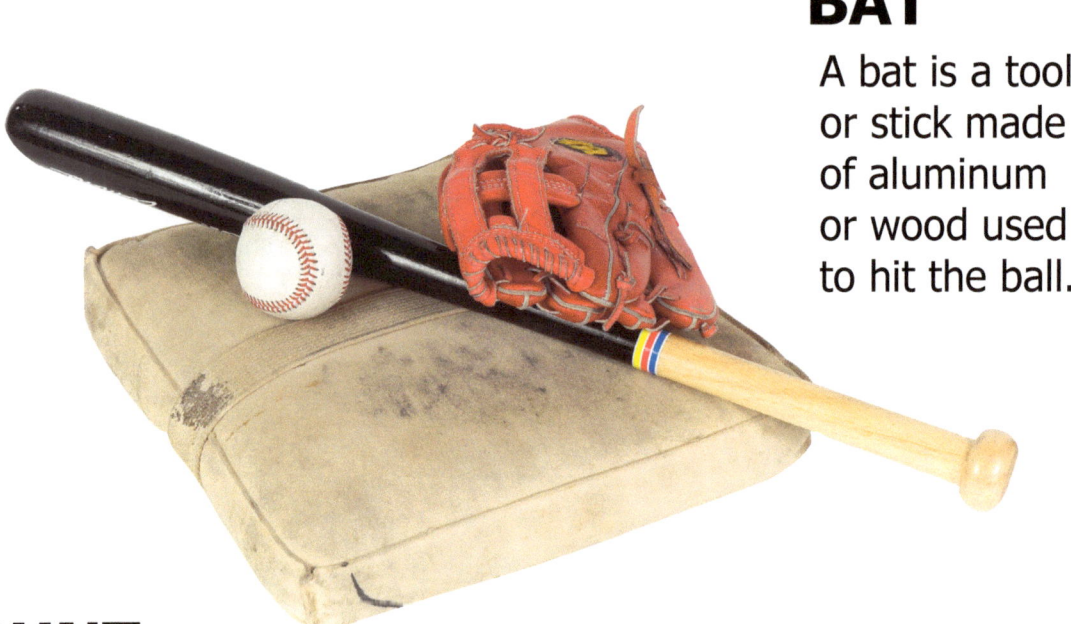

BUNT

A bunt is a softly hit ball where the batter taps the ball hoping to keep it in the infield. He does not swing at the ball.

BASE

There are three white canvas bags on the field that the runner must touch before crossing home plate to score a run.

CATCHER

The catcher squats behind the home plate and catches hard thrown balls from the pitcher while wearing protective gear and a face mask. He must have a strong throwing arm. He has to be able to throw a ball to catch runners who try to steal.

COACH

Coaches are responsible for training the team and setting up the batting order. He decides who plays which position and holds regular practices to make better players.

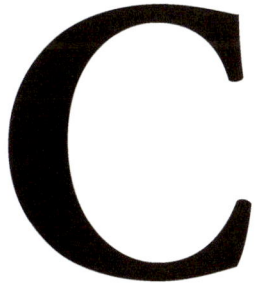

D

DIAMOND
The Diamond refers to the infield. This area is the space between the home plate, first, second and third bases. The area outside of home plate, first base and third base are marked with white lines referring to foul territory.

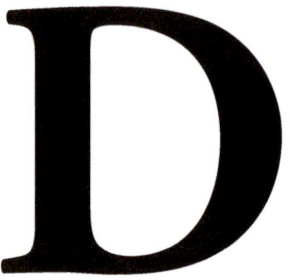

DUGOUT
This is the bench area where the players sit or stand while waiting their turn at bat. There are 2 dugouts, one for each team.

JERSEY, BAT & BALL MOUND

KNEE PADS, SHOES OR CLEATS, SOCKS, PANTS, CAP

BASES, GLOVE OR CATCHER MITT & CATCHER'S MASK

SHIN GUARDS & CHEST PROTECTOR

EQUIPMENT

All those things worn and used when playing the game of baseball are called equipment.

F

FOUL BALL

A ball hit by the batter which lands in the area outside of the first and third base lines is called a foul ball. The first and second foul balls are called a strike by the umpire. If the batter then bunts the ball and it goes into foul territory it also is called a strike and the batter is out.

GROUNDER

A hard hit ball that bounces, rolls, traveling close to the ground is called a grounder.

H

HOMERUN

A ball, sometimes called a homer, that is hit over the outfield fence allows the homerun hitter to run around all the bases and score. Any runners on bases ahead of the batter will also score.

INNING

An inning is a part of the game in which each team takes a turn at offense and defense. There are usually nine innings in a game.

INFIELD

The infield is the area in front of the three bases, first, second and third. With the home plate it forms a diamond shape.
 [See the letter "D"]

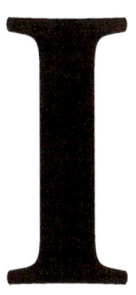

J

JERSEY

The jersey is another name for the shirt that a team wears to show what team they are on.

JUMBOTRON

The Jumbotron is the large video screen that is used in many of the large ball parks.

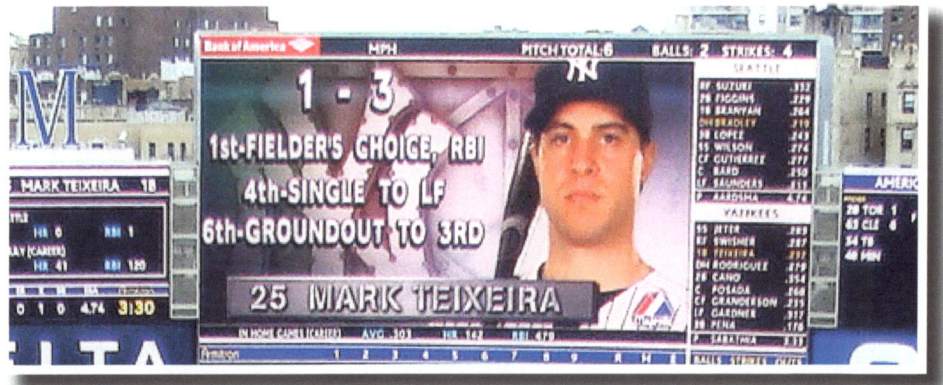

KNUCKLE BALL

A knuckle ball is a pitch that moves in an unpredictable manner. It dips and curves on its way to home plate. The pitcher grips the ball with his knuckles, giving it a different spin when thrown.

L

LEFT FIELDER
This is the player that covers the left field and tries to catch all potential homeruns.

LINE DRIVE
Line drive is a ball hit low, in a straight line through the air, directly to a fielder or through the infield.

MITT
A name for the leather protective hand covering, worn by the catcher and first baseman to help catch and handle the ball.

MOUND
The mound is an elevated area which the pitcher throws the ball from.

MANAGER
The Manager of a team tells the players what to do, how to play and teaches them that there is no "I" in Team.

M

NO HITTER
A no hitter is a game in which the pitcher has allowed no hits to any batter up at bat.

NAILED
The opposite of a no hitter. When a batter hits a homerun, it is said that he "nailed" the ball.

O

OFFICIALS
There are three officials in a game of baseball. One is towards the 1st base, one near the 3rd base and one is behind home plate.

OUTFIELDER
Outfielders are located in the right, left and center part of the field and are responsible to cover all balls that enter this area.

OUT OF BOUNDS
Any ball that is hit outside the sidelines is called "out of bounds" and is a foul ball.

OVERTHROW
A ball that is thrown out of the reach of another player has been overthrown.

PITCHER

The field player who stands on the pitcher's mound and throws balls to the catcher trying to get the batters out.

PROFESSIONAL

The player who plays baseball and is paid is called a professional and plays in one of many National Leagues.

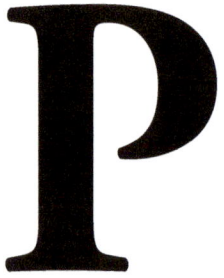

PLATE

The catcher and umpire stand behind the home plate. A runner must cross it to score a run.

P

QUICK PITCH

A quick pitch can be when the pitcher is throwing balls to walk the batter or a change of pace on the ball.

R

RIGHT FIELDER
The field player who covers the right side of the outfield.

RELIEF PITCHER
The pitcher who replaces the starting pitcher when he is removed from the game.

ROSIN
A dry powder which pitchers use to dust their hands for a better grip of the ball.

RUN
A run is when the player advances, touching each base and reaches home plate. One point is scored.

RULES OF THE GAME

- At the beginning of the game, nine players from the home or host team take the field as the defense team. It is called the bottom half of the inning.
- The guest team is at bat first and goes through their batting order until three outs are made. This is the top half of the inning.
- The pitcher starts the game by throwing the ball towards home plate and hopes it is in the strike zone.
- The strike zone is over the home plate between the batter's knees and his armpits. A pitch that goes through the strike zone is called a strike. A pitch that misses the strike zone is called a ball. Three strikes and the batter is out, four balls and the batter walks.
- If a batter swings and misses a ball, it is called a strike whether it goes through the strike zone or not.
- A pitch hit outside of the white foul lines is a foul ball. The first two fouls are called strikes. A third foul is not a strike unless the batter bunted the ball and it goes foul.
- A run is scored when the runner proceeds around the three bases touching each and crosses home plate without being tagged.
- On a tag play, the fielder must touch the base runner with the ball or his glove holding the ball before the runner reaches the base.
- On a force play, the fielder, with the ball, touches the base before the runner reaches the base. The runner is out.
- There are nine innings in the big leagues, the minor leagues and on the college levels. For Little League six innings are played and the number of innings can vary at different levels.

S STARTING ROTATION

Starting rotation has to do with the starting position of the teams starting pitchers.

SHORT STOP

The short stop is one of the four infield players who plays between second and third base.

SECOND BASEMAN

The player defends the second base and the right side of the diamond.

SAFE

If the runner touches the base before being tagged he is called safe by the umpire. If a baseman touches a base with the ball in his glove before the runner gets there, the runner is out.

SLIDE

When sliding into a base it is wise to slide feet first which sometimes helps to avoid being tagged. Also it might shake the ball out of the glove.

THIRD BASEMAN
The third baseman protects the third base and the left side of the diamond.

TEAM MANAGER
Team manager is the individual who manages the team and takes care of all details.

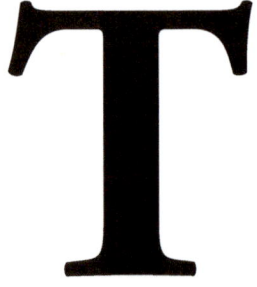

TRAVELING TEAM
Teams often travel distances to play other teams. They are called the visiting team.

U

UMPIRE
The umpire stands behind the catcher and calls balls and strikes. Like the catcher he wears a mask to protect himself from foul balls or wild pitches. Another referee is at first base calling balls fair or foul and runners out or safe.

V

VOLUNTEER

Volunteers are the backbone of all youth sports teams. They help with tranportation, taking care of equipment, and helping the team manager with all his tasks.

VICTORY
Winning means Victory!

VISITING TEAMS

It takes two teams to have a ball game so a visiting team comes in from another field to play.

WORLD SERIES - LITTLE LEAGUE
Many countries play in the Little League Baseball World Series. The players range in age from 11 to 13. See Wikipedia for more information & rules.

WILD PITCH
A wild pitch is a ball that is thrown so far from the strike zone, sometimes in the dirt, that the catcher can not catch or block it, allowing any base runner to advance a base.

WINNERS

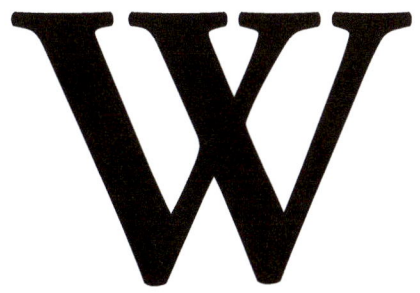

31

 **EXTRA INNINGS**

When the score is tied at the end of nine innings, extra innings are added and play continues until there is a winner. The home team finishes each inning by batting last. If the visiting team scores, the home team finishes the inning and if they do not tie or score more runs the game is over.

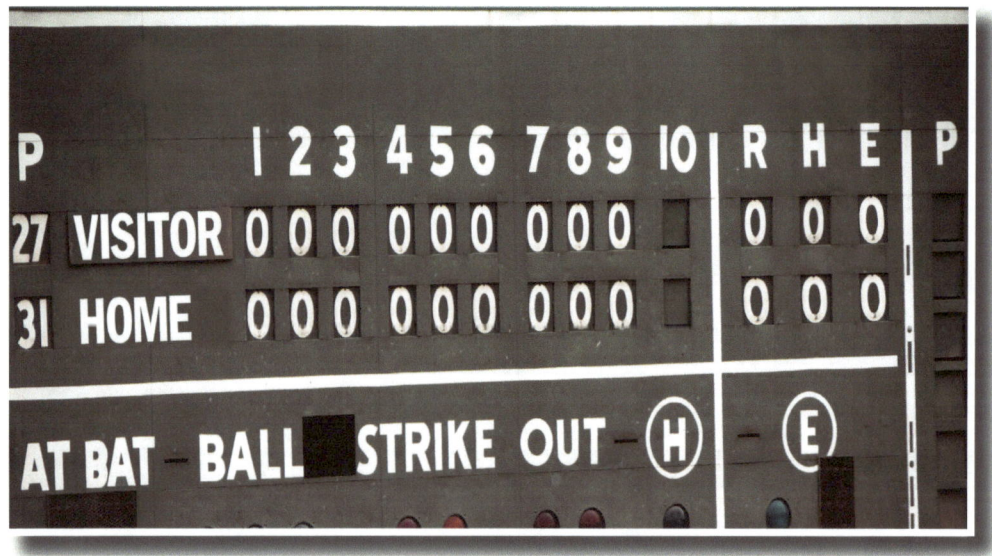

YANKEE STADIUM

The new Yankee stadium was built in 2009. Notice the Jumbatron at the back of the field.

YOUTH BASEBALL

Baseball is one of the many field sports played by boys and girls. Many start playing TEE ball only to graduate to Little League.

Z

STRIKE ZONE
The strike zone is the area over the home plate and between the knees and shoulders of the batter. If the pitcher puts the ball in this area, the umpire will call a strike whether the batter swings or not.

GLOSSARY OF BASEBALL TERMS

ALLEY
The section of the outfield between outfielders.

AROUND THE HORN
A double play going from third base to second base to first base.

ASSIST
Help from a fielder in putting an offensive player out. A fielder is credited with an assist when he throws a base runner or hitter out at a base.

AT BAT
The offensive team's turn to bat the ball and score. Each player takes a turn at bat until three outs are made.

BACKDOOR SLIDER
A pitch that appears to be out of the strike zone, but then breaks over the plate.

BACKSTOP
Fence or wall behind home plate.

BAG A base.

BALK (Call of Umpire)
Penalty for an illegal movement by the pitcher. The rule is designed to prevent pitchers from deliberately deceiving the runners. If called, baserunners advance one base.

BALL (Call of Umpire)
A pitch outside the strike zone.

BALTIMORE CHOP
A ground ball that hits in front of home plate (or off of it) and takes a large hop over the infielder's head.

BASEBALL
Baseball's core is made of rubber and cork. Yarn is wound around the rubber and cork centre. 2 strips of white cowhide are sewn around the ball. Official baseballs must weigh 5 to 5 1/4 ounces and be 9 to 9 1/4 inches around.

BASE HIT
A play in which the batter hits

the ball in fair territory and reaches at least first base before being thrown out.

BASE ON BALLS (Walk)
Four balls and the hitter advances to 1st base.

BASE COACH
A coach who stands by first or third base. The base coaches instruct the batter and base runners with a series of hand signals.

BASE LINE
The white chalk lines that extend from home plate through first and third base to the outfield and up the foul poles, inside which a batted ball is in fair territory and outside of which it is in foul territory.

BASES EMPTY
No runner on the bases.

BASES LOADED
Runners at each base.

BATTER
An offensive player who takes his position in the batter's box.

BATTER'S BOX
An area marked by white chalk lines on the left and right side of home plate in which a player must stand while batting.

BATTERY
Term referring to the pitcher and catcher combination.

BATTING ORDER
The offensive line-up of a team that lists the players who will bat. The batting order is given to the umpire before each game.

BOX SCORE
The progression of the game as written in a series of boxes indicating hits, runs, errors and player substitutions of each inning played.

BREAKING BALL
An off-speed pitch that curves.

BRONX CHEER
Crowd booing.

BRUSHBACK
A pitch that nearly hits the batter.

BULLPEN
Area designated for pitchers to warm-up. Generally consists of two mounds and two home plates.

CALLED GAME
A game suspended or ended by the umpire.

CAN OF CORN
An easy catch by the fielder.

CAUGHT LOOKING
When a batter is called out on strikes.

CATCHER'S BOX
Area behind home plate in which catcher must stand until the pitcher delivers the ball.

CELLAR
A team in last place.

CHANGE UP
A slow-pitch thrown with the exact arm action as a fastball, designed to disrupt the timing of the hitter.

CHECKED SWING
A partial swing. If the swing has gone more than halfway around, the umpire can rule it a full swing, or strike.

CHEESE
A good fastball.

CHIN MUSIC
A pitch that is high and inside.

CHOKE-UP
Gripping the bat up on the handle away from the knob of the bat.

CIRCUS CATCH
An outstanding catch by a fielder.

CLEAN-UP HITTER
Player who hits fourth in the batting order.

CLOSER
Relief pitcher who specializes in pitching the last few outs of a game. Generally used to hold a lead in the late innings of a game.

COMPLETE GAME
Statistical credit to a starting pitcher for pitching the entire

game.

COUNT
The number of called balls and strikes on a hitter.

CURVE
Pitch that moves down, across, or down and across, depending upon the rotation of the ball.

CUTTER (CUT FASTBALL)
A fastball with a late break on it.

CYCLE
When a batter hits a single, double, triple and homerun in the same game.

DESIGNATED HITTER
Player who bats in the pitcher's spot in the line-up. The Designated Hitter does not have a fielding position.

DINGER A homerun.

DONUT
Circular shaped weight that slides over the bat. The weight is used when a player is loosening up in the one deck circle.

DOUBLE
A hit that enables a batter to reach second base.

DOUBLEHEADER
Two games played back to back by the same teams.

DOUBLE PLAY
Any defensive play that results in two base runners being called out.

EARNED RUN
A run scored on a hit, walk or steal, without benefit from a defensive error on the play.

ERROR
Defensive mistake that allows a batter to stay at the plate or reach first base, or that advances a base runner.

FAST BALL
A straight pitch thrown by the pitcher as hard as possible.

FAIR TERRITORY
Part of the playing field within, and including the first base and third base lines, from home base to the bottom of the playing field fence and perpendicular upwards. All foul lines are in the fair territory.

FIELDER'S CHOICE
Term used when a fielder can chose among base runners or throw or tag out.

FIREMAN
A team's closer.

FLY BALL
Batted ball that goes high in the air in flights.

FORCE OUT
An out created when a runner is forced to advance because there is another runner behind them, although they will be thrown or tagged out. The defensive player needs only to touch the base being approached by the runner with the ball in hand to record the out.

FORKBALL
A pitch thrown by placing the ball between the first two fingers, usually resulting in a sinking ball.

FOUL LINE
Lines extending from home plate through 1st and 3rd base to the outfield fence and perpendicularly upwards. These lines are considered in play.

FOUL TERRITORY
Part of the playing field outside the first and third base lines extended to the fence and perpendicularly upwards.

FUNGO
A ball hit to a fielder during practice.

FUNGO BAT
Bat used to hit fungo. Usually longer and thinner than a regular bat.

GAP
The section of the outfield between the outfielders. Also called alley.

GOPHER
A ball hit for a homerun.

GRAND SLAM
A home run that is hit with a runner on every base. This hit scores 4 runs.

GREEN LIGHT
Signal from the coach to hit the next good pitch, or a signal to a base runner that gives the runner the authority to decide when to attempt a steal.

GROUNDER A ground ball.

GROUND BALL
A ball hit in the infield by the batter that bounces in the infield.

HEAT (HEATER)
A good fastball.

HIT
A play in which the batter safely reaches a base after hitting the ball, without aid from a fielding error or fielder's choice.

HIT AND RUN
Play-action situation in which the batter must swing at the pitch while the base runner attempts to steal the base.

HOME PLATE
The fourth station to be reached by the runner. The offensive team is credited with one run every time a player safely crosses this base. A pitched ball must cross the plate when thrown by the pitchers to be credited as a strike on the batter.

HOT CORNER Third base.

INFIELDER
Fielder who occupies a position in the infield. Most commonly refers to the first baseman, second baseman, third baseman, and shortstop.

INNING
A period of play. There are 9 innings in a regulation game, each team bats in an inning until they record 3 outs. The visiting team always bats in

the top half (beginning) of an inning. If the home team has a higher total after their opponents bat in the top half of the last schedule inning, the bottom half of the inning is not played and the score is final. A tie at the end of regulation play forces extra innings. The game continues until an inning is complete and the visitors have a higher score, or until the home team breaks the tie (then) they don't complete the 3 outs.

INTENTIONAL WALK
Four balls thrown on purpose to a batter advancing the hitter to first base. Generally, executed when 1st base is empty to set-up a force play.

KNUCKLE BALL
A pitch thrown by gripping one of the seams on a ball with fingernails and/or knuckles of the forefinger and middle finger with the thumb and other fingers underneath the ball. The ball is pushed out of the hand by the two fingers to keep the ball from rotating, causing the ball to move in an unpredictable manner.

LEFT ON BASE
Runners stranded on base after three outs.

LINE-UP
A team's batting order and fielding positions.

MENDOZA LINE
A batting average of around .200. Named after Pirate shortstop Mario Mendoza.

NO HITTER
A game in which a pitcher does not allow the opposing team to reach a base via a safe hit.

ON DECK
A term used to refer to the next batter up in the inning. This person stands in a designated circular area and warms up before batting.

OUT IN ORDER
Retiring the first 3 batters in an inning.

OUTFIELD
Area between the back edge of the infield and home run fence.

PASSED BALL
A pitched ball missed by the catcher, allowing a runner to advance.

PERFECT GAME
A game in which a pitcher does not allow any batter of the opposing team to reach base.

PICK OFF
An attempt by the pitcher to get a base runner out by throwing to the base from the stretch position.

PINCH HITTER
A hitter who substitutes in the line-up for a starting player. The original batter can't return to the game, so the pinch hitter or a third person takes over the defensive position as well.

PINCH RUNNER
A player entering the game to run for someone already on base.

PITCHOUT
When a pitch is thrown wide of the strike zone on purpose. A catcher will signal for a pitchout if they think that a runner is trying to steal.

PITCHING ROTATION
The order in which the starting pitchers take turns starting games, usually with three or four days rest between starts.

PULL HITTER
A batter that generally hits to the same side of the field that he bats. (eg, righthanded pull hitter hits to the left side of the field).

PUTOUT
In scoring, a fielder is credited with a putout if he receives the ball to put out a base runner or a hitter.

RUBBER
The pitching plate on the mound. The pitcher must have one foot connected to the plate while pitching to

the batter. The rubber is located 60' 6" (19.5 meters) from home plate.

RUN DOWN
A play used by fielders to tag out a runner caught between bases.

RUNS BATTED IN (RBI)
Statistics which shows how often a player has made it possible for their team mates to score while at bat. A player who has 30 RBI's has caused 30 runs to be score. A batter is not credited with an RBI if he hits into a double play or if the run is scored because of an error.

RUNNER
An offensive player who is advancing toward, touching, or returning to any base.

SACRIFICE BUNT
A bunt designed to advance a runner although the batter will be thrown out.

SACRIFICE FLY
Fly ball out that scores a runner from third base.

SAVE
A relief pitcher can be credited with a save if they can keep the team's lead while the opponent's tying or winning runs are on base, or if they pitch 3 or more innings without allowing the opponents to tie the game.

SCORING POSITION
Runner on second or third base.

SHUT OUT
A game in which one team doesn't score any runs.

SIGNS
1. Player signals given from the third base coach to the hitter and runner.
2. Hand signals given by the catcher to the pitcher suggesting the type of pitch to be thrown.

SINKER
A fast pitch that breaks downward as it reaches the homeplate.

SLIDER
A pitch that appears to the

batter as a fastball until it reaches the plate, then breaks sharply on a level plane. The ball is held similarly to the curve ball, but the wrist is kept straight, like a fastball, and broken downward.

SPIT BALL
Illegal pitch which a foreign substance (most commonly spit or grease) is applied to the ball causing it to react in an unpredictable manner.

STARTER
The pitcher who beings the game and pitches until he wins the game or is replaced by a relief pitcher.

STEAL
Attempting to advance a base between pitches without the batter hitting the ball or getting a base on balls.

STOLEN BASE
Successfully advancing a base between pitches without the batter hitting the ball or getting a base on balls.

STRIKE
A strike is called if a batter swings at a pitch and misses, or if the pitch simply passes through the strike zone. The first 2 foul balls that are not caught count as first and second strike. A foul ball that is not caught can never be counted as a third strike.

STRIKE OUT
Out recorded by recording three strikes on the batter.

STRIKE ZONE
The area over home plate between the batter's armpits and knees when the batter is positioned to swing. Any pitch that is delivered through this area is called a strike.

SUICIDE SQUEEZE PLAY
A play in which a runner on third breaks toward home on the pitch and the batter's responsibility is to bunt the ball allowing the runner to score.

SWITCH-HITTER
Player who is able to bat left-

handed or right-handed. A switch-hitter will bat from the opposite side in which the pitchers throws.

TAG
1. An action runners must perform before they can advance on a fly ball. Runners must touch the base they occupy after the ball is caught before they can try to advance. Runners can leave their base before a ball it hit, but must return and touch the base if the ball is caught. 2. An action executed when a defensive player touches a runner with the ball in an attempt to get them out.

TATER A homerun.

TEXAS LEAGUER
A bloop hit that drops between the infielder and outfielder.

TRIPLE
A hit enabling the batter to safely reach third base.

TRIPLE PLAY
A defensive play that records 3 outs.

TWO BASE HIT
A hit enabling the batter to safely reach second base. Also called a double.

UNCLE CHARLIE A curve ball

UTILITY PLAYER
A player who fills in in many positions.

WALK
An award given to the batter after the pitcher delivers 4 balls. If a hitter receives 4 balls during an at bat, they automatically advance to first base. Any forced base runners also advance. Also called base on balls.

WHEELHOUSE
A hitter's power zone.

WHIFF A strike out.

Stephanie Shriber Ellis always wanted to work with children, was graduated from Akron University and started her career as an early Elementary school teacher, in Lakewood, Ohio. She later taught in Erie, Pennsylvania where she opened the first private licensed Nursery School in the State.

She began writing books for children to help them develop a better understanding of the different terms connected with the sports they play and be able to feel comfortable utilizing them.

Using photographs with the alphabet letters, her books are a great introductory start to either tennis, soccer, baseball or the golf language. The books are fun, and inviting educational resources for children from six to twelve years of age. They help coach the children to discover the ins and outs of the sport regardless of when they begin to play.

Ms. Ellis lives in Florida with her family, two dogs and three feisty cats.

Other books written by Stephanie S. Ellis

MY PERSONAL SOCCER JOURNAL

An educational guide and record keeping journal for all children who play soccer. It is a fun and informative text starting when they begin their journey whether they are four, six, eight or twelve years old. It covers the different levels of soccer and gives both the children and the parents an introduction to the adventures ahead of them.

The SOCCER Alphabet Book

The SOCCER Alphabet book is a picture book for children from six to twelve years of age using the 26 letters of the alphabet and pictures to describe over 100 soccer terms and definitions. The pictures tell a story and help the children to understand soccer terms. It is a fun and educational book for all parents and children who love the game of soccer.

visit us at:
www.soccerpals.com
www.mackenziewoodspublishing.com

www.ingramcontent.com/pod-product-compliance
Lightning Source LLC
Chambersburg PA
CBHW041535040426
42446CB00002B/94